Authority

Foundations – Faith Life Essentials
Authority and Power of God's Word

ISBN 978-1-78263-536-9
Product code: B101D

Scripture quotations are from the New King James Version of the Bible, Thomas Nelson Publishers, Nashville, TN, © 1982.

This message is a transcript book, with added questions, remarks and study suggestions, edited by the Derek Prince Ministries editorial team.

Derek Prince Ministries
www.derekprince.com

EXPANDED
VERSION:
**GROUP
STUDY**

Authority
and Power of
God's Word

DPM

DEREK PRINCE MINISTRIES - UK

Contents

About This Study Series

The Bible is God's Word and our "instruction manual" to find the path to salvation in Jesus. It then shows us how to walk with Him once we have come to know Him. Logically, therefore, it is a hugely important part of our challenge as Christian believers to study the Word of God.

A sad fact is that very often we forget most of what we have heard quite quickly! As a result, what we have heard often has little impact on the way that we continue to live.

That is why we developed these Study Guides. As Derek Prince has said numerous times in his teaching, "It is a general principle of educational psychology that children remember approximately 40 percent of what they hear; 60 percent of what they hear and see and 80 percent of what they hear, see and do."

This Study Guide is intended to help you to assimilate the truths that you have heard into both your head and into your heart so that they become more than just knowledge and will begin to change the way that you live.

Living the Christian life

This study is part of a series of 10 messages, based on the doctrinal foundation of the Christian Life described in Hebrews 6:1-2 which says,

Therefore, leaving the discussion of the elementary principles of Christ, let us go on to perfection, not laying again the foundation of repentance from dead works and of faith

toward God, of the doctrine of baptisms, of laying on of hands, of resurrection of the dead, and of eternal judgment.

This mentions six specific foundation stones that we need to lay before we can build a dwelling place for the Lord in our hearts and lives:

1. Repentance from dead works
2. Faith towards God
3. The doctrine of baptisms – John's baptism, Christian baptism and baptism in the Holy Spirit
4. Laying on of hands
5. Resurrection of the dead
6. Eternal judgment.

When this teaching is applied in your life, with faith, we believe that it will deepen your relationship with God and enable you to live a truly successful Christian life.

How to Study

Each book contains a QR-code (or DVD) that links you to a talk by Derek Prince, the transcript of the talk and questions for personal application or to be discussed in a group setting.

Each video is about an hour long, divided in three parts. Set aside a reasonable length of time to read the Introduction, then watch or read Derek's teaching, and finally come back to the Study Guide to reflect on the Study Questions or to discuss them with your study group.

Once you have completed this series you will find that you have an excellent summary of the teaching. This will help you to share the content with others, whether to a friend, home group or congregation. The more you share the truths you are learning, the more they will become part of your own life and testimony.

Group Study

This study guide has been developed for use by small groups as well as by individuals.

Simply proceed through the material as a team, reflect on the questions and explore the statements together for a rich and rewarding experience.

Scripture to Memorize

In this book, we have chosen key Scriptures for memorization. They will relate in some way to your overall study. Memorizing them will place a spiritual sword in your hands which you, by the Holy Spirit, will be able to use in times of spiritual conflict.

The Word of God has supernatural power for those who will take the time and effort to "hide it in their hearts" by memorizing and meditating on it. As God's Word is hidden in your heart, it becomes constantly available to you for reference, comfort, correction and meditation. Put simply, it becomes part of your life.

Look up the verse in your own Bible and write it in the space provided. You will want to write and say this verse out loud several times until you are confident you know it well. Take time to meditate on the words and their application to your life. As a group, you could talk briefly about the meaning of the verse and its relevance to the lesson or share how you applied it.

You will be asked to recall your Memory Work at the end of the book.

SCRIPTURES TO MEMORIZE

Write down these verses and try to memorize them.

Hebrews 4:12

Proverbs 4:20-22

Authority and Power of God's Word – an Introduction

There are certain principles that need to be in place before we can actually lay a firm foundation for our faith. Our deepening relationship with Jesus, God's personal Word and the Bible, God's written Word, are essential in that process.

In this study you will learn about the importance of the Bible, the Word of God. "Where does Scripture's authority come from?"; "How much of the Scripture is relevant?", and "How can a book written by humans be perfect?" are all questions that Derek Prince is going to answer.

In addition, you are going to learn some of the wonderful uses and effects of Scripture in your life. Some of these seem too good to believe, but faith (or believing) is the place that you need to start because, "without faith it is impossible to please God" (Hebrews 11:6). Are you lacking that faith? Scripture has the answer for that too –Romans 10:17 says that "faith comes... by hearing, and hearing by the Word of God." If you don't have faith you can get it through God's Word.

Derek Prince shows from Scripture that God's provision for you is in His promises as revealed in His Word. Astonishingly, as you receive His Word, its effect is that you become a partaker of God's own nature.

Open your heart now to receive the truth of God's Word into your hearts and begin to enjoy its wonderful effects in your life.

Watch the Derek Prince video teaching *Authority and Power of God's Word* on YouTube. Scan the QR-code or visit dpmuk.org/foundations

This video has been divided into three sections, following the chapters in this book. You will find the links to these sections when you tap the 'down arrow' to expand the information about the video.

If you want to be completely and thoroughly equipped for every good work, the source of that preparation is Scripture.

The Author
of God's Word

In this study, you will examine the attributes of the Scripture, the Word of God—and especially its authority and power. As a beginning point, it will help you to consider the source and author of the Word—God Himself.

First, let's recognize that there are two different ways in which the title "the Word of God" is applied. Both the Bible and Jesus Christ are called "the Word of God." This brings out the fact that there is a complete identity between Jesus and the Bible. The Bible is God's written Word; Jesus is God's personal Word. If we really want to be rightly related to Jesus, we have to be rightly related to the Bible. We cannot be rightly related to Jesus but wrongly related to the Bible. This theme, then—the authority and the power of God's Word—is obviously of great importance to us.

The Author

If we stop to consider it, the word *authority* comes from the word *author*. In other words, it is the author who gives authority to whatever he produces. We need to know, therefore, who is the author of the Bible, the Scripture. The Bible itself clearly answers this question:

All Scripture is given by inspiration of God, and is profitable for doctrine, for reproof, for correction, for instruction in righteousness, that the man of God may be cwomplete, thoroughly equipped for every good work.
2 Timothy 3:16–17

If we want to be complete and thoroughly equipped for every good work, the source of that preparation is Scripture. Where Paul says that all Scripture is given by inspiration of God, the Greek word means "Godbreathed." In the Greek, the word for *breath* and the word for spirit are identical. That means all Scripture is inbreathed by the Spirit of God. In other words, the authority behind all Scripture is the authority of the Holy Spirit. He ultimately is the author. He used many different channels and many different instruments, but behind them all is the authority of the Holy Spirit who is God Himself. When we confront the Scripture, we confront the authority of God Himself.

God Inspired

The passage above says *all* Scripture is inspired—not some. Some people want to weed out the passages they regard inspired from those they do not consider really authoritative. But that is not in line with Scripture. The Holy Spirit Himself says all Scripture is inspired by God and all Scripture is profitable. In other words, no books can be left out or considered unimportant. Books like Ezra and Nehemiah are very important. The Song of Songs is very important. The prophet Nahum is very important. We must not just focus on a few well-known passages of Scripture and think that they are all that matters, because that is not correct. If we want to be equipped, we must be equipped by the whole Scripture. It will take us many years, but it is progressive. We can move from strength to strength (Psalm 84:7) as we meditate on, study and apply the Word of God. Remember that Jesus said building on His foundations is hearing and doing the Word of God. (See Matthew 7:24.) Not just hearing, but hearing and doing.

One Interpreter

As regards the interpretation of Scripture, there is only one author-ized interpreter—the Author Himself. There are quite a number of books bearing my name as the author. If anyone is not quite certain what they mean, I would be the best person to consult, because I know what I meant. I may not have said it as clearly as I should have, but I do know what I meant by what I wrote. If we want to know what any passage of Scripture means, we must likewise consult the Author. He is the only one who is authorized to interpret Scripture.

Peter says:

> *Knowing this first, that no prophecy of Scripture is of any private interpretation, for prophecy never came by the will of man, but holy men of God spoke as they were moved* [or borne along] *by the Holy Spirit.*
> *2 Peter 1:20–21*

No individual can interpret Scripture. Only the Holy Spirit is author-ized to do that. Peter agrees with what Paul pointed out: the authority behind the Scripture—the source of its inspiration—is the Holy Spirit.

The Fallibility of Man

We might reasonably say, "But the men that wrote the Bible were in many cases very weak and fallible. The Bible even records many of their sins." It is a mark of the accuracy of the Bible that it records the sins of the people who wrote it. A lot of people today would hush up their sins and not expose them, trying instead to present themselves as infallible. No author of the Bible does that. Even David, the author of most of the psalms, recorded his serious sins for all to read. How then can the Bible be infallible if the people that wrote it were fallible? We see a beautiful answer to that question in the Psalms:

The words of the Lord are pure words, like silver tried in a
furnace of earth, purified seven times.
Psalm 12:6

In that passage we see a picture of how people used to purify metal. They would build a furnace of clay, light a fire in it, and then put the metal in the furnace to be purified. We see there three elements in that picture:

1. the furnace of clay, which represents the human instrument,
2. the fire, which represents the Holy Spirit that purifies the silver, and
3. the silver, which is the message. That tells us how fallible men and women can be channels to produce an inspired and authoritative Word of God. The clay is the human vessel. The fire is the Holy Spirit. The silver, purified seven times, making it absolutely pure, is the message of God.

The number seven in the Bible links us to two realities: the Holy Spirit and perfection. Perfection is by the Holy Spirit. The Bible, though it came through vessels of clay—weak, fallible, sinful men and women—has been purified seven times by the fire of the Holy Spirit It is totally reliable.

Jesus and the Old Testament

To understand the authority and power of God's Word, we need to consider the attitude of Jesus Himself toward the Bible, because for us who are His disciples, He is the pattern. How did Jesus relate to the Bible? Let's look at a helpful Scripture in the gospel of John. In the context of a discussion with the Jewish leaders, Jesus said:

"If He [God] called them gods, to whom the word of God came
(and the Scripture cannot be broken) . . ."
John 10:35

In that one verse, Jesus gives to the Bible the two titles His followers have used ever since: "the Word of God" and "the Scripture." When Jesus identifies Scripture as "the Word of God," He means it proceeds from God. It did not proceed from man. It came from heaven—from God.

When He says "the Scripture," Jesus means that which has been recorded in writing. God said many things which are not recorded in writing, but those that are recorded in the Scripture— the Bible—are recorded for our special benefit. They contain all we need to know for our salvation.

Jesus' attitude toward the Bible is summed up in that phrase, "The Scripture cannot be broken." Nothing can express the authority of Scripture more completely than that simple phrase. If we believe that the Scripture cannot be broken, God will hold us accountable for it. He will expect us to accept the authority of Scripture in every area of our lives.

How Jesus Used Scripture

In regard to how we apply Scripture, here again, Jesus is our pattern. Let's look at what happened when Jesus was in the wilderness being tempted by Satan. The story begins at the end of Matthew chapter 3, beginning with the record of John the Baptist baptizing Jesus in the Jordan.

> *When He had been baptized, Jesus came up immediately from the water; and behold, the heavens were opened to Him, and He saw the Spirit of God [the Holy Spirit] descending like a dove and alighting [and remaining] upon Him.*
> *Matthew 3:16*

It is important for us to see that the Holy Spirit remained on Jesus, affirmed by the parallel Scripture in John 1:32–34:

> *And John bore witness, saying, "I saw the Spirit descending from heaven like a dove, and He remained upon Him. I did not know Him, but He who sent me to baptize with water said to me, 'Upon whom you see the Spirit descending, and*

remaining on Him, this is He who baptizes with the Holy
Spirit.' And I have seen and testified that this is the Son of God."

The Holy Spirit has descended on some of us at various times. But He has not always remained on us, because we have said and done things that made it so He could not remain. But Jesus never said or did anything that grieved the Holy Spirit or caused "the dove" to fly away.

After the baptism of Jesus, a voice came from heaven —the
voice of God the Father—saying: "This is My beloved Son,
in whom I am well pleased."
Matthew 3:17

We might be tempted to think that following such a wonderful pronouncement, Jesus was going to have a really easy time. After all, He now had the endorsement of both the Father and the Spirit, and the prophet John the Baptist. But that is not so.

The next step after the Father's announcement was Jesus being led out into the wilderness for forty days of fasting and temptation by Satan. Please do not imagine that God's blessing will always make life easy. In fact, in a certain sense, it may make life more difficult. Satan much more strongly opposes those whom God has anointed. Luke's gospel account says that Jesus was "led by the Spirit into the wilderness" (Luke 4:1), but at the end of the forty days Jesus returned "in the power of the [Holy] Spirit" (Luke 4:14). Those are two very different experiences. It is one thing to be led by the Spirit; it is another thing to move and operate in the power of the Spirit. And Jesus did not operate in the power of the Spirit until He had confronted Satan and won.

To some degree that truth applies to each one of us. We will have to overcome temptation and opposition in order to move in the power of the Holy Spirit. From the Matthew 4 account, we see that when the tempter came to Jesus, the first thing Satan tempted Him to do was to doubt. Nearly always, that is the initial approach of Satan. He will not immediately deny the Word of God, but he will question it. And he will cause us to doubt it. This has worked so many times in Church history that he has never had to find another tactic. But we must not let it work with us.

In Matthew 4, we read the first words Satan said to Jesus:

> *Now when the tempter came to Him, he said, "If You are the Son of God, command that these stones become bread."*
> *Matthew 4:3*

Remember, God had just spoken from heaven and said, "This is My beloved Son." But Satan was challenging Jesus to doubt what He had just heard from God by saying, "If you are the Son of God, then do something to prove it. Make these stones bread."

> *But [Jesus] answered and said, "It is written, 'Man shall not live by bread alone, but by every word that proceeds from the mouth of God.'"*
> *verse 4*

It is interesting to note that all the answers Jesus gave to Satan's three temptations were taken from the book of Deuteronomy. It is interesting, too, that neither Jesus nor the devil ever questioned the authority of the book of Deuteronomy. (So why should we waste our time doubting?) This is how Jesus dealt with each temptation: by meeting it with the written Word of God. We should never think that we are clever enough to argue with the devil. He is much more clever than we are, and he has been in this business a long time. We cannot convince him with our arguments, so we must meet him with the Scripture. Each time Jesus was tempted, He said, "It is written... it is written . . . it is written" (verses 4, 7, 10). Whenever Jesus said that, Satan changed the subject. The devil knew he had no answer to the Scripture. Don't be tempted to try to overcome Satan with philosophy or with theology. Just answer him with the written Word of God.

The Original Temptation

Jesus did not make the same mistake Eve made. At the beginning of human history in the first few verses of Genesis 3, we read:

> *Now the serpent* [who was Satan in bodily form] *was more cunning than any beast of the field which the Lord God had made. And he said to the woman, "Has God indeed said, You shall not eat of every tree of the garden'?"*
> *Genesis 3:1*

What did the serpent tempt Eve to do first? To doubt. And when doubt comes, the next step is disbelief. And when disbelief comes in, the next step is disobedience. Remember that well. We must never entertain doubt.

Eve made the mistake of thinking that she could meet the devil on his level. She gave him this answer: "We may eat the fruit of [every] tree"—she did not want to acknowledge that there were any restrictions—" but of the fruit of the tree which is in the middle of the garden," which was the tree of the knowledge of good and evil. Concerning that tree she said, "God has said, 'You shall not eat it, nor shall you touch it, lest you die'" (verse 3). Notice the devil's answer:

> *Then the serpent said to the woman, "You will not surely die."*
> *verse 4*

The devil begins by questioning, but he goes on to deny. A study of the last hundred years or more of Church history will reveal that wherever Satan has persuaded theologians or preachers to question the Scripture, he has always brought them to the point where they actually deny it. Don't start down that slippery downward path. The Scripture is authoritative. It is the Word of God. Accept it. Live by it. Answer the devil with it. He cannot answer the written Word of God. Paul says:

Take ... the sword of the Spirit, which is the word of God ...
Ephesians 6:17

There are two Greek words that are translated "word." One is *logos*. The other is *rhema*. Logos is the total, eternal counsel of God. Rhema is a spoken word of God. The word that is used in Ephesians 6:17 is rhema, the spoken Word of God. When you meet the devil, you have to meet him by speaking the Word of God. The Bible will not protect you if it is just sitting there on your bookshelf, or even if it is on your bedside table. The Bible only works when you quote it. You have to take it in your mouth and say it for yourself. Then it becomes a sharp, pointed sword from which the devil backs off. He has no answer for it.

Study Questions

1. What special insights did you gain from this lesson?

   ----

2. Why is studying the Bible important in growing in your Christian life? Some suggested Scriptures: Matthew 7:24-27, John 14:19-23, 1 John 2:4-5

   ----

3. People sometimes ask how the Scriptures could be written by sinful humans and yet still be perfect. How would you answer their question? Suggested Scriptures: 2 Timothy 3:16-17, Psalm 12:6

----

4. According to 2 Peter 1:20-21, who is the author of the Bible? Why is this important?

----

5. When considering the importance of Scripture, a good question to study is how Jesus viewed the Old Testament (since the New Testament had not yet been written). How did Jesus relate to the Bible? (John 10:35)
How did He apply Scripture? (Matthew 4:1-10)

----

6. Read Genesis 3:1-8. What did Satan tempt Eve to do in the garden of Eden? What was the result?
   In what situations are you (or have you been) tempted to doubt God's Word? What promises from the Bible do you find hard to trust?

   ----

7. Our response to Satan's temptation to doubt God, should not be to argue with him. Rather, how should we respond?

   ----

8. God's Word is eternal and speaks to us today. How would you respond when people say the Bible is outdated? (see also Matthew 22:31-32)

   ----

9. Reflect/discuss: God's blessing will not always make life easy. Satan much more strongly opposes those whom God has anointed.

----

10. According to 2 Timothy 3:16-17, all Scripture is inspired by God – not some. If we want to be equipped, we must be equipped by the whole Scripture. We can be tempted to only read well-known passages from the Bible. Is there a book from the Bible that you have never read yet? Commit yourself to reading it this week or month.

As you finish the first part of this study, ask for God's help to apply the truths from this study practically in your life.

SUMMARY

- Both the Bible and Jesus Christ are called "the Word of God." The Bible is God's written Word; Jesus is God's personal Word. If we really want to be rightly related to Jesus, we have to be rightly related to the Bible.

- The authority behind all Scripture is the authority of the Holy Spirit. He ultimately is the author.

- The Holy Spirit is not only the Author behind the Scriptures but also the Interpreter (2 Peter 1:20–21)

- If we want to be equipped, we must be equipped by the whole Scripture.

- Jesus said the Scripture cannot be broken. (John 10:35)

- Satan tempts us to doubt God's Word. He will question it and cause us to doubt it. (Matthew 4:1-4, Genesis 3:1-10)

- Jesus dealt with each temptation by meeting it with the written Word of God.

- The Word of God is the Sword of the Spirit. (Ephesians 6:17) We use this sword by speaking God's Word out loud.

The authority behind
the writings of the
apostles is the authority
of the Holy Spirit.

Authority of God's Word

Let's look at what Jesus says about the authority of the written Word of God. Remember from our earlier section where we saw that the word Scripture means "God's Word in writing." Jesus said:

> *"Do not think that I came to destroy the Law or the Prophets* [that is the Jewish way of speaking about the Old Testament]. *I did not come to destroy but to fulfill. For assuredly, I say to you, till heaven and earth pass away, one jot or one tittle will by no means pass from the law till all is fulfilled."*
> Matthew 5:17–18

Jot in modern Hebrew (yodh), is the smallest letter in the Hebrew alphabet, and a *tittle* is just a little curve added to a letter in writing to distinguish it from a similar letter. They are the two smallest items in written Scripture's text, and Jesus said not one of them will ever pass away. This statement clearly indicates that Jesus acknowledged the absolute authority of the written Word of God. He was not talking about the spoken Word of God at that point, because the words jot and tittle apply only to that which is written. Jesus absolutely endorsed the total authority of the written Word of God.

A little further on, quite near the end of His ministry, Jesus was dealing with the Sadducees. These people were the liberals of that day, the people who did not accept the authority of all Scripture. In fact, they only accepted the authority of the first five books, the Pentateuch.

They were challenging the teaching that there will be a resurrection of the dead, and they came to Jesus with a smart question. But here is how Jesus answered them:

> *"But concerning the resurrection of the dead, have you not read what was spoken to you by God, saying, 'I am the God of Abraham, the God of Isaac, and the God of Jacob'? God is not the God of the dead, but of the living."*
> Matthew 22:31–32

Notice how Jesus applied that Scripture. The words He quoted were written by Moses about fourteen centuries earlier. They were actually words spoken by the Lord directly to Moses. But Jesus did not speak about them as something that was said to Moses fourteen centuries ago. Instead, He said, "Have you not read what was spoken to you by God?" How Jesus presented the Word of God in this matter reveals something very powerful to us today. The Scripture is never out of date. It is never just the record of human cleverness. Even if it was written 3,000 years ago, it is still God speaking to us today. That is the authority of Scripture as Jesus understood it.

Scripture Fulfilled

In addition to understanding how Jesus understood and utilized Scripture, we need to consider how the very life of Jesus fulfilled the Scripture. If we were to go through the entire New Testament, we would find eighteen different places where it says the same words. In regard to particular events in the life of Jesus, it says "that the Scripture might be fulfilled." In other words, not merely did Jesus believe the Scripture. Not merely did He proclaim the Scripture, He also obeyed the Scripture. His whole life was the outworking of Scripture.

We could look at many aspects of His life that affirm this truth. However, for our purposes in this booklet, I will provide just four specific references for further study. These concern His birth, His human life, His death and His resurrection. Concerning each of these, the Bible says the event took place "that the Scripture might be fulfilled." (See Matthew 1:22; 12:27; 27:35; Luke 24:44.) Jesus could not have more strongly endorsed the authority of Scripture than to do so with the very events of His life.

The Authority behind Scripture

As we study passages in the New Testament, let's address an important question. What is the authority behind the New Testament? You may be surprised to learn it is the same authority as that which is behind the Old Testament. Particularly, we will look at two passages in which Jesus spoke to His disciples. In the first of these passages, Jesus is taking leave of His disciples. He is preparing them for the fact that He is going to leave.

> *"These things I have spoken to you while being present with you. But the Helper, the Holy Spirit, whom the Father will send in My name, He will teach you all things, and bring to your remembrance all things that I said to you."*
> *John 14:25–26*

The authority behind the writings of the apostles is the authority of the Holy Spirit. Jesus said the Holy Spirit would help them in two ways: First, whatever Jesus had not taught them, the Holy Spirit would teach them. Second, whatever Jesus had said that might have been forgotten by them, the Holy Spirit would bring it to their remembrance. The record of the gospels does not depend on human memory—it depends on the truth of the Holy Spirit.

A little further on, Jesus brings out the same truth again. He says to His disciples:

> *"I still have many things to say to you, but you cannot bear them now. However, when He, the Spirit of truth, has come,*

He will guide you into all truth; for He will not speak on His
own authority, but whatever He hears He will speak; and He
will tell you things to come."
John 16:12–13

Let me point out that Jesus breaks the laws of grammar to empha-size that the Holy Spirit is not an *it* but a *he*. According to Greek gram-mar, Jesus should have said *it*, but He didn't. He said *He*. In other words, the Holy Spirit is not just an it, He is a person. And we need to relate to Him as such. Again Jesus affirms an encouraging truth: whatever teaching we need that we have not yet received will come to us by the Holy Spirit. As we go on in this same passage, the next verse says:

"He [the Holy Spirit] *will glorify Me, for He will take of what is*
Mine and declare it to you."
verse 14

Let me point out another extremely important mark of the Holy Spirit in this passage. He always glorifies Jesus. If you are ever con-fronted by spiritual manifestations that do not glorify Jesus but give glory to a man or some other entity, you can be sure that spirit is not the Holy Spirit. The supreme ministry of the Holy Spirit is to reveal and glorify Jesus.

The Bible instructs us to test the spirits (1 John 4:1), and this is one good way of doing so. One sure way to test if a work or a word is from the Holy Spirit is to ask: Will it glorify Jesus? If it does not—no matter how good or spiritual it may sound, or how loud and resounding the message—it is not from the Holy Spirit. He will not glorify anyone but Jesus. The moment human personalities begin to take glory to them-selves, the Holy Spirit says, "Sorry, but I have to leave. You can carry on, but I won't be here."

Over the years, we have seen many ministries which have gone astray on this point. I could not count the number of ministries that have ended in ruin because men took the glory which the Holy Spirit will only give to Jesus. We need to be personally very conscious of that ourselves. We need to continually examine ourselves to see if we are giving the glory to Jesus or trying to persuade people that Derek Prince or any of us is someone important. Derek Prince is a sinner saved by the grace of God—and the same is true of each of us. Jesus is the only One worthy to receive the glory. And reminding us of that truth is one of the Holy Spirit's primary roles.

The Nature of God's Word

Let's go on now to a really interesting and important theme: the nature of God's Word. In Hebrews we find an analysis of the nature of the Word of God:

> *For the word of God is living and powerful, and sharper than any two-edged sword, piercing even to the division of soul and spirit, and of joints and marrow, and is a discerner of the thoughts and intents of the heart.*
> *Hebrews 4:12*

Again, we notice that the Word of God is compared to the sword, as we pointed out in our earlier examination of Ephesians 6:17. The Word is a sword.

Further, the Word of God is not dead, it is living. The Word of God is not just black marks on white paper. It is not just sounds that come from a preacher's mouth. It is alive. It is living. And wherever it comes, it brings life. The Word of God is alive and powerful. Thank God, it is powerful. It is more powerful than all the lies with which Satan has filled the world. And the Word of God is the ultimate answer.

Next, we read of the effects of the Word of God upon us. The passage says: "Piercing even to the division of soul and spirit." This is very interesting. The Bible reveals that man is a triune being: spirit, soul and body. In truth, man is a triune being created in the likeness of a triune God: Father, Son and Holy Spirit. But the only way we can learn to distinguish between the soul and the spirit is by the Word of God. It is the only instrument sharp enough to penetrate and separate what is soulish from what is spiritual.

This is very important, because as we study the New Testament, we find that the soulish, in many ways, is in opposition to the spiritual. In 1 Corinthians 2, for instance, Paul says the soulish man does not receive the things of the Spirit of God, for they are spiritually discerned. (See verse 14.) So, it is important that we learn to distinguish between what is spiritual and what is soulish. But only the Word of God can do that. The Word of God can also divide between the joints and the marrow. In other words, the Scripture can penetrate where no surgeon's scalpel can and where no psychiatrist's probing can penetrate. It is the only agent that takes us right into the very depths of human personality.

In the next part of this revealing passage, we see that the Word of God is "a discerner of the thoughts and intents of the heart." To discern means to analyze, to see into the very nature of something. Someone once said, many years ago when I was a young believer (and it has always stuck with me), "Remember, when you're reading your Bible, your Bible is also reading you." It is a two-way transaction. This has always been so vivid to me, because I started to read the Bible simply as a professional philosopher treating it as a work of philosophy. At first, when I began reading, I found it very dreary. Only my determination that no book would ever defeat me kept me reading. But as I read, I discovered that I began to feel quite different about myself. Up to that time, I thought I had the answer to everything— that philosophy could provide a solution to everything. But as I went on reading the Bible, I became less and less self-confident. I could not understand what was happening to me. I thought I was getting old before my time—although I was not even twenty-five years old. I did not realize that while I was reading the Bible, the Bible was reading me. At the end of the process, I felt like Belshazzar at his feast when the writing appeared on the wall: "You have been weighed in the balances, and found wanting" (Daniel 5:27). My self-conceit, pride, arrogance, and intellectual assurance all began to wilt before the Scripture. Even though I did not yet believe the Bible at the time, it was still doing its work. Bear in mind that when you read your Bible, your Bible is also reading you.

The Word Works in Us

For one further aspect of what the Bible will do, let's look in 1 Thessalonians. Paul is writing to the believers in Thessalonica who had responded in a wonderful way to the message of the gospel. He says to them:

> *For this reason we also thank God without ceasing, because when you received the word of God which you heard from us, you welcomed it not as the word of men, but as it is in truth, the word of God, which also effectively works in you who believe. 1 Thessalonians 2:13*

What the Bible will do in you depends, in part, on how you receive it. If you receive it as the word of man, it will not work its full work in you. But, if you receive it as the Word of God, it works effectively in you. When you read your Bible, take time every now and then to say to the Lord, "I believe this is Your Word. I receive it as Your Word. Let it work in me everything You have sent it to do, in every area of my being—spirit, soul and body—because I believe it."

Everything We Need

Peter made one of the most remarkable statements found anywhere in Scripture. The apostles wrote rather long sentences, and this truth comes right in the middle of a sentence. (In English, we usually have to divide them up.)

> *… His [God's] divine power has given to us all things that pertain to life and godliness, through the knowledge of Him*

who called us by glory and virtue ...
2 Peter 1:3

That is an amazing statement! It says that God's divine, omnipotent power has already given to us everything we are ever going to need! You might respond, "Well, God, I don't seem to have it. Where is it?" The next verse tells us:

. . . by which have been given to us exceedingly great and
precious promises, that through these you may be partakers
of the divine nature, having escaped the corruption that is in
the world through lust.
verse 4

We see from this passage that God has given to us all things we need for life and godliness. They are in the promises. I have coined this sentence: "The provision is in the promises." So if we want to receive all that God has provided, we have to receive it through His promises, because in them is everything we are ever going to need.

Partakers of God's Nature

In addition to His promises, the provision also comes through the knowledge of Jesus, because the Scripture reveals Jesus. And here is the amazing statement. (If this were not so clearly written in the Bible, I would not dare to say it.) It is through partaking of the promises that we can be partakers of the divine nature, having escaped the corruption that is in the world through lust. We need to be very careful here, because there is a lethal kind of teaching which is very fashionable today. This teaching is that if you go on long enough and do the right things, you can become a god. You may have encountered that teaching yourself. It is called New Age teaching. Incorporating a lot of Hindu philosophy and Eastern thought, the New Age philosophy teaches that if you go on long enough you can become a god. (The Mormons teach the same, not publicly at first, but sooner or later.) I want to tell you, that is obviously false. Here is one basic reason. God is uncreated; we are created. The created can never become uncreated. It is a deception. But we can become partakers of the nature of God as we receive and apply the promises. I always think of Jacob's ladder in this regard. You may remember the dream Jacob had. He was out in the desert by himself and he went to sleep with his head pillowed on a stone. While Jacob slept he had a vision—a dream of a ladder reaching to heaven. The foot was on the earth, the top of the ladder was in heaven and the angels of God were ascending and descending. And Jesus Himself was at the top of the ladder, and He spoke to Jacob in the dream. The Bible, in a sense, is like Jacob's ladder. Every promise is one rung on the ladder. Every time you appropriate a new promise, you go one step higher. Ultimately, it will take you to heaven. Never neglect your Bible. It is the key to your well-being and the key to your success. It is the most precious gift God has ever given us.

Let's bear in mind that we have so many Bibles today. We discuss whether we will use this translation or that one, whether we want it illustrated or with notes. But let's remember that there are millions of people in the world today who have never once opened a Bible. They have no choice. Remember also that in previous centuries men and women laid down their lives in sacrifice to preserve the Bible for you and me. Let's treat it with reverence. Let's be respectful to the Bible because it is one of the many ways that God comes into our lives.

Study Questions

1. What do we mean when we talk about "the authority of God's Word" in our lives? How do you demonstrate the authority of God's Word in your life?

   ----

2. Are there specific situations in your life or in your family where you need to apply the Word of God? They might be spiritual problems (need for salvation, deliverance, freedom from a particular habit, revelation in a specific situation), physical problems, financial problems, relational problems, etc. What specific Scripture answers the need you wish to overcome? How can you practically apply it?

   ----

3. How can you be sure the Bible, and especially, the New Testament, is really the inerrant Word of God and not merely man's ideas about what Jesus said? (See also John 16:12-13, 2 Timothy 3:16-17, Hebrew 4:12)

----

4. Read John 14:25-26. What role does the Holy Spirit play in understanding Scripture?

----

5. There are many different Bible translations. Which is your favorite and why? Pray for ministries that translate the Bible into new languages.

----

6. The Holy Spirit always glorifies Jesus. Ask the Holy Spirit to make this your personal aim in life. Let Him show you anything that is not honoring Jesus at this point and what is keeping you from glorifying Him.

----

7. Discuss/reflect: What the Bible will do in you depends, in part, on how you receive it. (See 1 Thessalonians 2:13) In what ways can we receive it?

----

8. According to 2 Peter 1:3-4, we are partakers of God's nature. Explain in your own words what this means. What does it mean to you personally?

----

9. By the Word of God we can learn to distinguish between the soul and the spirit. Why is that important? (See 1 Corinthians 2:14, Hebrews 4:12)

....

....

....

....

As you finish the first part of this study, ask for God's help to apply the truths from this study practically in your life.

SUMMARY

- Jesus acknowledged the absolute authority of the written Word of God. (Matthew 5:17–18)

- The Scripture is never out of date. Even if it was written three thousand years ago, it is still God speaking to us today.

- The record of the gospels does not depend on human memory—it depends on the truth of the Holy Spirit. (John 14:25–26)

- The Word of God is alive and powerful. It is more powerful than all the lies with which Satan has filled the world. And the Word of God is the ultimate answer. (Hebrews 4:12)

- The only way we can learn to distinguish between the soul and the spirit is by the Word of God.

- What the Bible will do in you depends, in part, on how you receive it. If you receive it as the Word of God, it works effectively in you. (1 Thessalonians 2:13)

- If we want to receive all that God has provided, we have to receive it through His promises, because in them is everything we are ever going to need. It is through partaking of the promises that we can be partakers of the divine nature, having escaped the corruption that is in the world through lust. (2 Peter 1:3-4)

If you never seriously apply the Word of God, you will never become mature.

3

The Effects of God's Word

Let's now deal with a very exciting topic: the effects of God's Word. As we saw previously, Paul said to the Thessalonians that the Bible works effectively in us because we believe it (1 Thessalonians 2:13). So I want to point out nine effects that God's Word can have in our lives— nine aspects of what God's Word will do for us.

1. Faith

We will look, first of all, in Romans:

> *So then faith comes by hearing,*
> *and hearing by the word of God.*
> *Romans 10:17*

That is a wonderful Scripture. It is especially meaningful for me because at one time I lay in a hospital for one year in the deserts of North Africa with a skin disease that the doctors could not heal in that climate. They eventually called it chronic eczema. (Actually, they still do not have a cure for that disease even today.) I had just newly become a Christian and I kept saying to myself, "I know if I had faith God would heal me." And then the next thing I always said was, "But I don't have faith." There I was in what John Bunyan calls, in Pilgrim's Progress, "the slough of despond"—the valley of despair. Then one day a brilliant ray of light shone into that dark valley. It came from

Romans 10:17:

"So then, faith comes . . ." If you don't have faith, you can get it. You need not stay without it. Faith comes . . . by hearing the Word of God. In the time of the New Testament, the majority of people read out loud, even if they were by themselves. For instance, we know that the Ethiopian eunuch was in his chariot reading from the prophet Isaiah and Philip heard him read, even though he was reading to himself. (See Acts 8:26–39.) There is something to be said about reading out loud, because when you hear yourself read, faith comes. That is the number one product of the Scripture.

2. New Birth

It is by the Word of God that we are born again. James, speaking about God, says:

> *Of His own will He brought us forth by the word of truth*
> [the Bible], *that we might be a kind of firstfruits of*
> *His creatures.*
> *James 1:18*

Do you know why God did it? Because He decided to do it. We get no further explanation than that. When we go back to the beginning, it all starts with God's decision. God decided to bring forth a people for Himself, and He decided they would be brought forth by the Word of God, the Scripture. That is what brought you and me to know God. That is what caused us to become a new creation, the people of God. It was the Word of God.

Then Peter goes on with the same theme:

> *Since you have purified your souls in obeying the truth*
> *through the Spirit in sincere love of the brethren, love one*
> *another fervently with a pure heart, having been born again,*

not of corruptible seed but incorruptible, through the word of
God which lives and abides forever.
1 Peter 1:22–23

Notice that you purify your soul by obeying the truth. Not by hearing the truth, but by obeying it. The result will be sincere love. The incorruptible seed is the seed of God's Word. When it is received into the heart by faith, it produces the new birth. The seed is incorruptible; the life it produces is incorruptible. The nature of the seed determines the nature of the life that comes from it. If you plant an apple pip, you do not get an orange tree. The nature of the seed determines the nature of the life. The Word of God is incorruptible, and the life it produces is incorruptible. It is divine, holy, eternal.

3. Spiritual Nourishment

Once you have been born again, what you need is nourishment. The marvelous thing is that God's Word has provided suitable nourishment for every stage of spiritual growth. When you are just a little spiritual baby, you need milk. That is what Peter says in the next chapter:

As newborn babes, desire the pure milk of the word,
that you may grow thereby.
1 Peter 2:2

Once you are born again, you should have a very healthy appetite for the Word of God. Most Christians can testify that when they were born again the one thing they wanted to do was read the Bible. We are born again as healthy infants with a healthy appetite for the one thing that can really nourish us. Then as we grow up, we need things like bread. Jesus said to Satan when Satan tempted Him to make bread out of stones:

*"Man shall not live by bread alone, but by every word that
proceeds from the mouth of God."*
Matthew 4:4

God's Word is not only milk, but it is also bread. As we grow up we
need still more solid food, and this also is provided.

In Hebrews chapter 5 the writer is addressing Jewish people who
had a knowledge of the Scripture from their background. He is tell-
ing them what God might wish to say to some of us: "You should be
doing better than you are." They had the knowledge of the Scripture,
but they were not using it.

*For though by this time you ought to be teachers, you need
someone to teach you again the first principles of the oracles
of God; and you have come to need milk and not solid food.*
Hebrews 5:12

What was the evidence of their immaturity? They couldn't digest
more than the very simplest, basic truths.

*For everyone who partakes only of milk is unskilled in the
word of righteousness, for he is a babe. But solid food belongs
o those who are of full age [mature], that is, those who by reason
of use have their senses exercised to discern both good and evil.*
verses 13–14

In order to mature, you have to exercise your senses. You have to
practice. You have to apply the Word of God, you have to use it to recognize the situations you find yourself in and the forces that you are
dealing with. That is the way to maturity. If you never seriously apply
the Word of God and if you do not live by the Word of God, you will
never become mature. You will never be able to take more than milk
or maybe just a little bread. But solid food is only for those who have
practiced. It is for those who have exercised— who have applied the
Word diligently and regularly in their lives.

4. Mental Illumination

In Psalm 119, a familiar verse to many, the psalmist, speaking to God, says:

> *The entrance of Your words gives light, It gives understanding*
> *to the simple.*
> *Psalm 119:130*

The entrance of God's Word into your mind and into your heart gives light. This is different from education. You can be educated and totally in the dark. How do I know? Because I was highly educated, yet totally in the dark until the light of the Word of God shone into my life. Remember that education is not light. Years ago I was dealing with African students in East Africa whose one ambition was to get an education. At one point, I wrote a little tract for them called: "You are seeking education, but are you also finding wisdom?" I pointed out that wisdom and education are not the same. I also pointed out a fact which has shocked some people: most of the trouble in the world is caused by educated fools. Theodore Roosevelt, former president of the United States, once said, "If a man is a thief, he will steal a railroad car, but if you educate the same man he'll steal the whole railroad!" Please bear in mind, education

is a useful thing. But it is not light. In fact, as I say, some of the most educated minds are in the deepest darkness. It is only the entrance of God's Word that gives light.

5. Physical Healing

God's Word provides physical healing—something I can say out of my own personal experience. Let's begin by looking at Psalm 107:

> *Fools, because of their transgression,*
> *And because of their iniquities, were afflicted.*
> *Psalm 107:17*

Did it ever occur to you that some of us are afflicted because we have been leading a wrong life? Over the years many people have come to me for prayer for healing. Very rarely have they recognized that the source of their problem is their wrong living. However, Scripture says that fools, because of their transgressions and iniquities, are afflicted.

> Their soul abhorred all manner of food,
> And they drew near to the gates of death.
> Then they cried out to the Lord in their trouble,
> And He saved them out of their distresses.
> He sent His word and healed them,
> And delivered them from their destructions.
> verses 18–20

The people mentioned here were at the point of death. The doctor could do no more for them. My comment is that people often put off prayer until it is very late. The people described in Psalm 107 were at death's door, and suddenly it occurred to them it might help to pray. As a result, God sent His Word and healed them. Notice, there are three things God does when He sends His Word: He saves, He heals and He delivers. The three great acts of God's mercy—saving from sin, healing from sickness and delivering from demon power—are accomplished primarily through His Word. Many Christians are looking to find some preacher who will lay hands on them and pray for them to get healed. It may well happen. Many people have come to me, thinking that if I pray for them they will be healed. But they aren't. In fact, my concern became that they might really be looking to Derek Prince and not to the Lord. But let me tell you this: you can be healed without any preacher if you will receive God's Word—for He sent His Word and healed them, and delivered them from their distresses.

Here is my favorite verse, which got me out of the hospital when no medication would do it: Proverbs 4:20–22. This is in the King James Version, because that is how I first read it:

My son, attend to my words;
incline thine ear unto my sayings.
Let them not depart from thine eyes;
keep them in the midst ofthine heart.
For they are life to those that find them, and health
to all their flesh. KJV

God's words, he says, will be health to all our flesh. There I was. I had been in the hospital about seven months. The doctors were not healing me, and I was saying, "If only I had faith, I know God would heal me." Then I got to the Scripture I mentioned earlier: "Faith comes by hearing, and hearing by the Word of God." I began to hope. Then I began to look through the Scripture again with a new hope. However, I had a problem. I had been a professional philosopher, and the job of philosophers is to make simple things complicated. So, I just could not take the Word of God in its simplicity. I read promise after promise about God healing, but I thought, "That only means He heals my soul. He's not really interested in my body—that is corrupt. It is going to die anyhow." For instance, when I would read, "Bless the Lord, O my soul . . . who forgives all your iniquities, who heals all your diseases" (Psalm 103:1, 3), I would say, "That could only mean my soul's diseases." But when I got to Proverbs 4:20–22, I could no longer get around it. In that passage God clearly says His words are "life to those that find them, and health to all their flesh." My response to that was, "Not even a philosopher can make flesh mean anything but flesh. God's Word is health to my whole physical body." When I looked at the note in the margin, the alternative reading for health was "medicine." I happened to be what the army called a medical orderly. I said to myself, "How do people take their medicine?" The answer? Three times daily, after meals. So that is what I did. Over a period of three or four months I took God's Word as my medicine three times daily after every meal. The result God gave me from reading and believing the Word was complete and permanent healing and health in one of the most unhealthy climates in the world—the Sudan.

6. Victory over Sin and Satan

In Psalm 119, the psalmist takes us right to the heart of the whole question of a life of purity and victory:

> *How can a young man cleanse his way?*
> *By taking heed according to Your word.*
> *Your word I have hidden [stored up] in my heart,*
> *That I might not sin against You.*
> *Psalm 119:9, 11*

Many young people today question whether it is really possible to lead a pure life. Most of their educators will tell them it isn't. Some of those educators will recommend what they call "safe sex," which is never safe. But the Bible says a young man who gives attention to his way according to the Word of God can lead a pure life. I thank God that when I worked among the African young people I saw those words fulfilled time and time again. These people were made pure and they led clean lives because they gave heed to the Word of God. Someone once said: "Either sin will keep you from the Bible, or the Bible will keep you from sin."

> The psalmist gives this testimony:
> *Concerning the works of men, By the word of Your lips,*
> *I have kept away from the paths of the destroyer.*
> *Psalm 17:4*

There is a weapon that will deal with the devil—the sword of the Spirit. As Ephesians 6:17 says, "Take . . . the sword of the Spirit, which is the word of God." When we take the sword—God's Word—and begin to use it in faith, it gives us supernatural wisdom and authority. Do you remember what we looked at earlier in Matthew 4? When Jesus encountered Satan, He met him with only one weapon: "It is written."

7. Cleansing and Sanctification

Paul addresses the following words to husbands. However, the main thrust of what he is saying is not just about human husbands relating to their wives, but about the relationship of Christ, as the bridegroom, to His bride, the Church. Paul tells us two very important provisions that Christ (as Savior and Lord and bridegroom of the Church) has made for the Church.

> *Husbands, love your wives, just as Christ also loved the church and gave Himself for her, that He might sanctify and cleanse her with the washing of water by the word, that He might present her to Himself a glorious church, not having spot or wrinkle or any such thing, but that she should be holy and without blemish.*
> *Ephesians 5:25–27*

The first provision of Christ is that He has redeemed us by His blood for Himself. But there is something further: that He might cleanse us and sanctify us with the washing of water with the Word. The Word of God sanctifies us and it cleanses us. John said of Jesus, "This is He who came by water and blood" (1 John 5:6)—not by water only, but by blood. By the blood of His sacrifice, He redeems us. But by the water of His Word, He cleanses and sanctifies us. We need both. We are redeemed by the blood that we might be cleansed by the Word.

8. Our Mirror

In the epistle of James, we read these words about the work God's Word does in us, and how we are to receive His Word:

> *Therefore putting aside all filthiness and all that remains of wickedness, in humility receive the word implanted, which is able to save your souls. But prove yourselves doers of the word, and not merely hearers who delude themselves.*

For if any one is a hearer of the word and not a doer, he is like
a man who looks at his natural face in a mirror; for once he
has looked at himself and gone away, he has immediately
forgotten what kind of person he was. But one who looks
intently at the perfect law, the law of liberty, and abides by it,
not having become a forgetful hearer but an effectual doer,
this man shall be blessed in what he does.
James 1:21-25 NASB

When God's Word comes to us, we have two obligations: to receive it with humility and to act on what it says. James uses the example of a mirror. He says that when we read the Word of God and allow ourselves to be confronted by it, it is like a mirror held up in front of our eyes. It shows us what we are really like—not our external appearance, but our inward nature and character. James points out that when you look into a natural mirror, if you see there is something wrong, the sensible thing to do is tend to it. If your hair is out of order, you brush it. If your face is dirty, you wash it. You act on what you see in the mirror. The same is true when you look into the mirror of the Word of God. You need to see your spiritual self in it and act on whatever it shows you that you need to do. Here is an encouraging perspective as we look into that mirror:

[God] made him [Jesus] who had [or knew] no sin to be sin for
us, so that in him we might become the righteousness of God.
2 Corinthians 5:21 NIV

Because of Jesus, when we look in the mirror, we do not see ourselves in our sinful condition. Instead we see ourselves with the righteousness of God that has been imputed to us through faith in Christ.

9. Our Judge

Judgment is not something we like to think about, but the fact of the matter is that judgment is a part of God's total dealings with the human race. Furthermore, in the last resort, the final judge is God Himself. This is clearly presented throughout the whole Bible. God is presented as the final judge of the whole human race. Someday we are all going to answer to God. We see this truth in a number of passages in Scripture. Let's look at a few of them:

> May the Lord, the Judge, render judgment today...
> Judges 11:27
> Surely He is God who Judges in the earth.
> Psalm 58:11

> If you call on the Father, who without partiality judges according to each one's work, conduct yourselves throughout the time of your stay here in fear . . .
> 1 Peter 1:17

We have to face this fact: there is judgment, and the ultimate judge of all is God. The Scripture reveals that there is a divine order of judgment: God has His plan for how judgment is going to take place. Stated very simply, God the Father is the judge, but He has made Jesus the judge. And Jesus, in turn, has made the Word the judge. Let's see how the Father has delegated the judgment to the Son. Jesus says:

> "For the Father judges no one, but has committed all judgment to the Son, that all should honor the Son just as they honor the Father. He who does not honor the Son does not honor the Father who sent Him."
> John 5:22–23

God the Father gave authority to Jesus the Son to execute judgment because He is the Son of Man. He did this for two reasons: so that all should honor the Son as they honor the Father and because Jesus is the Son of Man. Not only is Jesus the Son of God, but He is also the Son of Man. As the Son of Man, He understands us—our weaknesses, our frailties, and our temptations. He is a just and merciful judge because He shares our nature. We also need to understand this truth: the Son has delegated His authority as judge to the Word. Jesus explains:

> *"And if any one hears My sayings, and does not keep them, I do not judge him; for I did not come to judge the world, but to save the world. He who rejects Me, and does not receive My sayings, has one who judges him; the word I spoke is what will judge him at the last day."*
> *John 12:47–48 NASB*

Ultimately, the judge we will have to face is not the Father, nor the Son. It will be the Word. There is one element to this matter of judgment that we need to consider: judging ourselves. In 1 Corinthians, Paul gives us a very practical application. Speaking about people who have incurred God's judgment by partaking unworthily of the Lord's Communion, Paul says we do not need to suffer that kind of judgment upon ourselves. But if we judged ourselves rightly, we should not be judged. (1 Corinthians 11:31)

We can escape God's judgment if we will judge ourselves. How? By looking into the mirror of the Word of God, accepting what it shows us and realizing that it is not only a mirror but also our judge. Humility, repentance, and obedience to the Word of God deliver us from the fear of judgment. The Bible speaks about "the answer of a good conscience," which is required of us as we profess our faith in Christ through baptism (1 Peter 3:21). How can we have the answer of a good conscience? As we see the requirements in the Word of God and apply those standards to our lives. As a result, we no longer need to fear the judgment of God. We have judged ourselves by the Word; therefore, we do not have to face God's judgment on our lives.

As we conclude this study, let me just recapitulate those nine effects of God's Word:

1. The Word of God produces faith.
2. It is the seed of the new birth.
3. It provides spiritual nourishment.
4. It produces mental illumination.
5. It provides physical healing.
6. It makes victory over sin and Satan possible.
7. It provides cleansing and holiness.
8. It is a spiritual mirror.
9. It is our ultimate judge.

Let us apprehend the significance of the authority and power of God's word by restating the truths we discovered along the way, and then praying for God to help us walk in those truths.

"I affirm that if I receive the Bible as the word of man, it will not work its full work in me. But, if I receive it as the Word of God, it works effectively in me. When I read my Bible, I will take time every now and then to say to the Lord, 'I believe this is Your Word. I receive it as Your Word. Let it work in me everything You have sent it to do, in every area of my being— spirit, soul and body—because I believe it'."

PRAYER

Dear Lord, thank You for the provision of Your Word. Please help me to understand it, absorb it, make it part of my life, and walk in it in a way that brings glory to You and to the name of Jesus. For it is in that precious name I pray. Amen."

Study Questions

1. Meditate on the Parable of the Sower in Matthew 13:1-23. What are some of the "rocks' which can prevent God's Word from growing in your heart?

   ----

2. What is the difference between wisdom and education? How is wisdom obtained? Is it possible to be knowledgeable in the Scriptures and still not have wisdom? Explain.

   ----

3. Describe (or share) personal experiences where you had to use the Word of God to defeat Satan or to overcome a temptation.

----

4. You will only experience the power of God's Word to the degree you are able to apprehend the truths of the Scriptures by faith. Reflect on the nine effects of God's Word. Do you experience any hindrances to accept and apply these truths by faith? Take time to pray about it.

----

5. Faith comes by hearing the Word of God. When you read your Bible, have you ever tried reading it out loud to yourself? Describe your experience. Consider a one-week trial to read the Bible out loud whenever you read it.

----

6. Read 1 Peter 1:22-23. You purify your soul by obeying the truth, not by hearing it. Why?

----

7. Proverbs 4:20-22 states that the Word of God is health (or medicine) to all our flesh. Write down any thoughts and prayers that come to mind when you read these verses.
    Derek Prince responded to this verse by taking God's Word as a 'medicine', three times a day. What do you think of his approach?

As you finish the first part of this study, ask for God's help to apply the truths from this study practically in your life. Remember to thank God for every new revelation that He shows you and to receive it with gladness. Here is a prayer to help you:

PRAYER

Dear Father, I want to thank You for showing me the true importance of the Bible. I ask that You would forgive me for not giving it the top priority in my life and pray that You would empower me to change.

Thank you for giving me the Holy Spirit who, as the Author, has complete knowledge and authority of the Scriptures and will guide me into all truth, teach me all things and bring to my memory those things that You have said at the moment that I need them.

Please help me to grow in my familiarity of Your Word so that when Satan comes to tempt me, I can use Scripture as an impermeable defense. As I seek to love You more, please help me to love and revere Your Word.

Lord Jesus, I recognize You as the personal Word of God and that my attitude to the Bible reflects my attitude to You. I have come to see some of the wonderful benefits of receiving Your Word into my spirit, soul and body, allowing it to have its full effect. Today I proclaim my desire for You in personal and written form – help me to come into line with Your Word and to become more and more like You. Amen.

SUMMARY

There are nine main effects of God's Word as we receive it by faith:

- It produces faith. (Romans 10:17).

- It is the seed of the new birth - Incorruptible seed produces incorruptible life (1 Peter 1:22–23, James 1:18)

- We receive spiritual nourishment: Milk (1 Peter 2:2); Bread (Matthew 4:4) and solid food (Hebrews 5:12–14)

- We receive mental illumination (Psalm 119:130) – education in itself is not light. Wisdom comes through God's Word.

- We prepare ourselves to receive physical healing. (Psalm 107:17–20, Proverbs 4:20–22)

- It gives us victory over sin and Satan. (Psalm 119:9, 11 and Matthew 4:4, 7, 10)

- Cleansing, sanctification and holiness. (Ephesians 5:25–27)

- The Bible acts as a spiritual mirror. (James 1:23–25)

- God's Word is our judge.

In the next study, *Through Repentance to Faith*, you will examine what it means to have faith and why repentance needs to come before faith.

Recall and write down the verses you memorized
at the beginning of this book:

Hebrews 4:12

Proverbs 4:20-22

About the Author

Derek Prince (1915–2003) was born in India of British parents. He was educated as a scholar of Greek and Latin at Eton College and King's College, Cambridge in England. Upon graduation he held a fellowship (equivalent to a professorship) in Ancient and Modern Philosophy at King's College. Prince also studied Hebrew, Aramaic, and modern languages at Cambridge and the Hebrew University in Jerusalem. As a student, he was a philosopher and self-proclaimed agnostic.

Bible Teacher

While in the British Medical Corps during World War II, Prince began to study the Bible as a philosophical work. Converted through a powerful encounter with Jesus Christ, he was baptized in the Holy Spirit a few days later. Out of this encounter, he formed two conclusions: first, that Jesus Christ is alive; second, that the Bible is a true, relevant, up-to-date book. These conclusions altered the whole course of his life, which he then devoted to studying and teaching the Bible as the Word of God.

Discharged from the army in Jerusalem in 1945, he married Lydia Christensen, founder of a children's home there. Upon their marriage, he immediately became father to Lydia's eight adopted daughters – six Jewish, one Palestinian Arab, and one English. Together, the family saw the rebirth of the state of Israel in 1948. In the late 1950s, they adopted another daughter while Prince was serving as principal of a teacher training college in Kenya.

In 1963, the Princes immigrated to the United States and pastored a church in Seattle. In 1973, Prince became one of the founders of Intercessors for America. His book Shaping History through Prayer and Fasting has awakened Christians around the world to their responsibility to pray for their governments. Many consider underground translations of the book as instrumental in the fall of communist regimes in the USSR, East Germany, and Czechoslovakia.

Lydia Prince died in 1975, and Prince married Ruth Baker (a single mother to three adopted children) in 1978. He met his second wife, like his first wife, while she was serving the Lord in Jerusalem. Ruth died in December 1998 in Jerusalem, where they had lived since 1981.

Teaching, Preaching and Broadcasting

Until a few years before his own death in 2003 at the age of eighty-eight, Prince persisted in the ministry God had called him to as he traveled the world, imparting God's revealed truth, praying for the sick and afflicted, and sharing his prophetic insights into world events in the light of Scripture. Internationally recognized as a Bible scholar and spiritual patriarch, Derek Prince established a teaching ministry that spanned six continents and more than sixty years.

He is the author of more than fifty books, six hundred audio teachings, and one hundred video teachings, many of which have been translated and published in more than one hundred languages.

He pioneered teaching on such groundbreaking themes as generational curses, the biblical significance of Israel, and demonology. Prince's radio program, which began in 1979, has been translated into more than a dozen languages and continues to touch lives. Derek's main gift of explaining the Bible and its teaching in a clear and simple way has helped build a foundation of faith in millions of lives. His nondenominational, nonsectarian approach has made his teaching equally relevant and helpful to people from all racial and religious backgrounds, and his teaching is estimated to have reached more than half the globe.

DPM Worldwide Ministry

In 2002, he said, "It is my desire – and I believe the Lord's desire – that this ministry continue the work, which God began through me over sixty years ago, until Jesus returns." Derek Prince Ministries International continues to reach out to believers in over 140 countries with Derek's teaching, fulfilling the mandate to keep on "until Jesus returns." This is accomplished through the outreaches of more than thirty Derek Prince offices around the world, including primary work in Australia, Canada, China, France, Germany, the Netherlands, New Zealand, Norway, Russia, South Africa, Switzerland, the United Kingdom, and the United States.

For current information about these and other worldwide locations, visit **www.derekprince.com.**

FOUNDATIONS
faith life essentials

www.dpmuk.org/shop

This book is part of a series of 10 studies on the foundations of the Christian faith.

Order the other books to get everything you need to develop a strong, balanced, Spirit-filled life!

1. Founded on the Rock

There is only one foundation strong enough for the Christian life, and we must be sure our lives are built on Jesus Himself.

2. Authority and Power of God's Word

Both the Bible and Jesus Christ are identified as the Word of God. Learn how Jesus endorsed the authority of Scripture and how to use God's Word as a two-edged sword yourself.

3. Through Repentance to Faith

What is faith? And how can you develop it? It starts with repentance: to change the way we think and to begin acting accordingly.

4. Faith and Works

Many Christians live in a kind of twilight - halfway between law and grace. They do not know which is which nor how to avail themselves of God's grace.

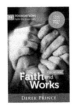

5. The Doctrine of Baptisms

A baptism is a transition - out of an old way of living into a totally new way of living. All of our being is involved. This study explains the three different forms of baptism presented in the Bible.

6. Immersion in the Spirit

Immersion can be accomplished in two ways: the swimming pool way and the Niagara Falls way. This book takes a closer look at the Niagara Falls experience, which relates to the baptism of the Holy Spirit.

7. Transmitting God's Power

Laying on of hands is one of the basic tenets of the Christian faith. By it, we may transmit God's blessing and authority and commission someone for service. Discover this Biblical doctrine!

8. At The End of Time

In this study, Derek Prince reveals the nature of eternity and outlines what lies ahead in the realm of end-time events.

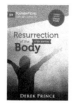

9. Resurrection of the Body

The death and resurrection of Jesus produced a change in the universe. Derek explains here how the resurrection of Jesus impacted man's spirit, soul, and body.

10. Final Judgment

This book examines the four major, successive scenes of judgment in eternity. Exploring the distinctive aspects of these four judgments, Derek opens the Scriptures to bring forth treasures hidden there.

Christian Foundations Course

If you have enjoyed this study and would like to deepen your knowledge of God's Word and apply the teaching – why not enrol on Derek Prince's Christian Foundations Bible Course?

Building on the Foundations of God's Word

A detailed study of the six essential doctrines of Christianity found in Hebrews 6:1-2.

- Scripture-based curriculum
- Practical, personal application
- Systematic Scripture memorisation
- Opportunity for questions and personal feedback from course tutor
- Certificate upon completion
- Modular based syllabus
- Set your own pace
- Affordable
- Based on Foundation Truths for Christian Living

For a prospectus, application form and pricing information, please visit www.dpmuk.org, call 01462 492100 or send an e-mail to enquiries@dpmuk.org

Foundational Truths For Christian Living

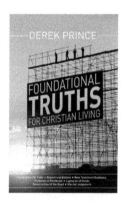

Develop a strong, balanced, Spirit-filled life, by discovering the foundations of faith: salvation; baptism, the Holy Spirit, laying on hands, the believers' resurrection and eternal judgment.

Its reader-friendly format includes a comprehensive index of topics and a complete index of Scripture verses used in the book.

ISBN 978-1-908594-82-2
Paperback and eBook
£ 13.99

www.dpmuk.org/shop

More best-sellers by Derek Prince

- Blessing or Curse: You can Choose
- Bought with Blood
- Life-Changing Spiritual Power
- Marriage Covenant
- Prayers & Proclamations
- Self-Study Bible Course
- Shaping History Through Prayer and Fasting
- Spiritual Warfare for the End Times
- They Shall Expel Demons
- Who is the Holy Spirit?

For more titles: www.dpmuk.org/shop

Inspired by Derek's teaching?

Help make it available to others!

If you have been inspired and blessed by this Derek Prince resource you can help make it available to a spiritually hungry believer in other countries, such as China, the Middle East, India, Africa or Russia.

Even a small gift from you will ensure that that a pastor, Bible college student or a believer elsewhere in the world receives a free copy of a Derek Prince resource in their own language.

Donate now: www.dpmuk.org/give
or visit www.derekprince.com

Derek Prince Ministries

DPM–Asia/Pacific
38 Hawdon Street
Sydenham
Christchurch 8023
New Zealand
T: + 64 3 366 4443
E: admin@dpm.co.nz
W: www.dpm.co.nz

DPM–Australia
15 Park Road
Seven Hills
New South Wales 2147
Australia
T: +61 2 9838 7778
E: enquiries@au.derekprince.com
W: www.derekprince.com.au

DPM–Canada
P. O. Box 8354 Halifax
Nova Scotia B3K 5M1
Canada
T: + 1 902 443 9577
E: enquiries.dpm@eastlink.ca
W: www.derekprince.org

DPM–France
B.P. 31, Route d'Oupia
34210 Olonzac
France
T: + 33 468 913872
E: info@derekprince.fr
W: www.derekprince.fr

DPM–Germany
Söldenhofstr. 10
83308 Trostberg
Germany
T: + 49 8621 64146
E: ibl@ibl-dpm.net
W: www.ibl-dpm.net

DPM-Netherlands
Nijverheidsweg 12
7005 BJ, Doetinchem
Netherlands
T: +31 251-255044
E: info@derekprince.nl
W: www.derekprince.nl

Offices Worldwide

DPM–Norway
P. O. Box 129
Lodderfjord
N-5881 Bergen
Norway
T: +47 928 39855
E: sverre@derekprince.no
W: www.derekprince.no

Derek Prince Publications Pte. Ltd.
P. O. Box 2046
Robinson Road Post Office
Singapore 904046
T: + 65 6392 1812
E: dpmchina@singnet.com.sg
W: www.dpmchina.org (English)
    www.ygmweb.org (Chinese)

DPM–South Africa
P. O. Box 33367
Glenstantia
0010 Pretoria
South Africa
T: +27 12 348 9537
E: enquiries@derekprince.co.za
W: www.derekprince.co.za

DPM–Switzerland
Alpenblick 8
CH-8934 Knonau
Switzerland
T: + 41 44 768 25 06
E: dpm-ch@ibl-dpm.net
W: www.ibl-dpm.net

DPM–UK
PO Box 393
Hitchin SG5 9EU
United Kingdom
T: + 44 1462 492100
E: enquiries@dpmuk.org
W: www.dpmuk.org

DPM–USA
P. O. Box 19501
Charlotte NC 28219
USA
T: + 1 704 357 3556
E: ContactUs@derekprince.org
W: www.derekprince.org

Lightning Source UK Ltd.
Milton Keynes UK
UKHW021657130720
366461UK00005B/144